All Kinds of Bible Puzzles

by Brenda Chester Johnson

STANDARD PUBLISHING
Cincinnati, Ohio

3.99

To my wonderful girls, Angela and Stephanie.

The Standard Publishing Company, Cincinnati, Ohio
A division of Standex International Corporation
© 1995 by Brenda Chester Johnson

02 01 00 99 98 97 96 95   5 4 3 2 1

ISBN 0-7847-0319-1

Contents

Generations

Persons of diverse backgrounds and circumstances were ancestors of Christ. Match the correct descriptor with the appropriate ancestor of Christ.

DESCRIPTOR	ANCESTOR
1. Killed Goliath	A. Solomon
2. Father of Hebrews	B. Rehoboam
3. Son of Judah and his daughter-in-law, Tamar	C. Boaz
4. Wisest king of Israel	D. David
5. Father of David	E. Salmon
6. Ten tribes of Israel revolted during his reign	F. Asa
7. Husband of Ruth	G. Joseph
8. Third king of Judah	H. Abraham
9. Husband of Mary	I. Perez
10. Married Rahab, the prostitute	J. Jesse

Siblings (Half or Otherwise)

Families of the Bible often had children that were related by several relationships. Match the sister or brother with his or her sibling.

1. Abraham	A. Joseph
2. Solomon	B. Nahor
3. Seth	C. Shem
4. Martha	D. Jesus
5. Esau	E. Asahel
6. Ishmael	F. Cush
7. Benjamin	G. Adonijah
8. Miriam	H. Jacob
9. James	I. Leah
10. Rachel	J. Abel
11. Ham	K. Nadab
12. Perez	L. Michal
13. David	M. Eliab
14. Jonathan	N. Isaac
15. Joab	O. Zerah
16. Canaan	P. Lazarus
17. Eleazar	Q. Moses

It's About Africa

Match the following person or place with the appropriate descriptor. Each item represents some feature of African descent or knowledge.

PERSON/PLACE	DESCRIPTOR
1. Zerah	A. Queen of Ethiopia, Acts 8:27
2. Simon of Cyrene	B. Ethiopian wife of Moses, Exodus 2:21
3. Libya	C. Ethiopian king defeated by Judah's king Asa, 2 Chronicles 14:9
4. Candace	D. Egyptian mother of Ishmael; first son of Abraham, Genesis 16:15
5. Zipporah	E. Helped bear Christ's cross
6. Asenath	F. Ethiopian who saved Jeremiah, Jeremiah 38:7-12
7. Jarha	G. Referred to as mingled people, Ezekiel 30:5
8. Kedar	H. Egyptian wife of Joseph; Manasseh and Ephraim's mother, Genesis 41:45, 50-52
9. Hagar	I. Egyptian slave married to Sheshan's daughter, 1 Chronicles 2:35
10. Ebed-Melech	J. Son of Ishmael, Genesis 25:13

Animals, Animals, Animals

```
P E E H S R M E A G L E M S L I O N
P I G E O N O I M D S D W W E M D N
T U Y Z H O W L S A N C G A O O U G
U G D O V E D M N E V A R N P M Q R
N R S M P O B T G B W P M D A R A E
I A N M O B W M O G A M E L R D S Y
C G A S X C P N A C M P G F D C S H
O Y I W B A N T E L O P E G J O T O
R P L A N E W O V G N E M E O M P U
N W E L Q S R A E B H O O P S A W N
D V U L T U R E B E R E I R K R T D
S G P O I V E C J F O X F P E F O E
P Q U W Z L N R A M D J F J R N G H
A H E N E A G Q C W R L W L O O W P
R C P S E N U S K F A B C W L G C B
R D A P C A I M A C G F I S H S T S
O E V U I T U E L F O B W B L G H C
W M N L X R D O G S N P J F R O G S
```

WORD LIST

ANTELOPE	GOAT	RAM
BEARS	HEN	RAVEN
CALF	HORSE	SCORPION
CAMEL	JACKAL	SHEEP
DOGS	LAMB	SNAIL
DOVE	LEOPARD	SPARROW
DRAGON	LION	SWAN
EAGLE	OWLS	SWALLOW
FISH	OX	UNICORN
FOX	PIGEON	VULTURE
FROGS	PYGARG	WEASEL
GREYHOUND	QUAIL	

Spreaders of the Word

```
U N X H A B A K K U K T H N I S K J R
D H B L P W J I A T S L N Y Z V O P Q
Y S E G M G S S I F C A E E H R M Z
T O P J H A L Q Y L A T M A N D J R A
J R H C I U F A A R O N Q U Z S N T F
M Z T A Q Y D S W P M G U Y E L I C W
H Y H E C A J H O S E A R S U L C T K
A P W R G I H W I B Q I O U B I F M O
N U Y H T C M L R Y P M A H I J A H D
O B J Q R A K O D D I J C L H A L S A
J S C Y H H A I M E R E J I Y G U B Z
S M U H A N U F E W D T N A T H A N M
```

WORD LIST

AARON	JEHU	JONAH
MOSES	AMOS	JOEL
SAMUEL	JOHN	HOSEA
NATHAN	HABAKKUK	AHIJAH
ZADOK	JEREMIAH	ISAIAH
NAHUM	IDDO	MICAH

Fiery Furnace

```
V R E Q S A E I D A T O B X F O A
G S W S U B C J L E C I W S X U Y
Y E B C L E N J T P C Z F D M P L
J V F K L D A E R F E R V J E G E
T G E E Q N R G C S P S E D S B B
C B N C X E E D Y H B F U E H T T
H A G T Y G V X P A O W E V A A A
R B F Z B O I K R D U V L X C E U
O Y L R W D L B U R N I N G H H N
F L A M E E E M O A D E T A E H E
A O M K G O D K F C R E V I L E D
J N E N D W O R S H I P C I D O L
R S A E U O F M T Y P X O J L Q O
E N N E B U C H A D N E Z Z A R G
V B S E V E N B O G N I K L A W V
O I E Q K L D N C B A W F T D Q J
N K Y N K C H A L D E A N S I T O
```

WORD LIST

WALKING	CHALDEANS
ABEDNEGO	BOUND
SHADRACH	DELIVERANCE
MESHACH	NEBUCHADNEZZAR
BABYLON	FLAME
WORSHIP	HEATED
IDOL	SEVEN
BURNING	HEAT
ANGEL	FOUR
GOLDEN	COATS
DELIVER	DECREE
GOD	

Water, Water, Seas, and Rivers

```
R  G  E  R  E  V  I  R  E  L  I  N  S  I  E
A  B  A  N  A  G  I  H  O  N  L  E  W  U  H
A  B  C  L  T  N  O  W  O  R  E  R  P  H  N
K  R  A  N  I  G  O  Z  A  N  H  H  V  E  D
U  P  N  P  V  L  T  L  D  E  R  A  M  I  E
F  T  O  O  I  V  E  M  J  A  S  N  J  H  A
B  R  N  B  N  O  S  E  T  H  I  O  A  I  D
K  E  E  A  H  E  Y  E  N  T  R  N  B  D  S
G  I  C  L  D  U  S  T  M  L  A  R  B  D  E
C  L  S  E  Z  R  R  J  T  K  L  A  O  E  A
H  M  U  H  I  H  O  A  R  A  P  J  K  K  D
E  Z  E  V  O  U  L  J  O  Y  E  I  R  E  Y
B  L  E  N  L  N  R  Z  M  P  A  L  S  L  S
A  R  A  F  L  M  P  H  A  R  P  A  R  O  I
R  G  N  R  E  D  S  E  A  K  J  C  U  Y  N
```

WORD LIST

GOZAN	CHEBAR
ABANA	KISHON
GIHON	EUPHRATES RIVER
NILE RIVER	GALILEE
PISON	KANAH
DEAD SEA	JABBOK
RED SEA	ARNON
PHARPAR	HIDDEKEL
JORDAN	

Things Addressed in the Bible

```
R S T P R M T N G C O M F O R T E B T H
E H T I A F V R V P G C B D D P T A A I
S S E R S R S E A Y B I L I E R I C T N
U B A B E V T E R N W E T V H A S K S G
R B S V D W B I T A S R E I D Y T S D S
R V C S H X W U N R I L T N L E I L N A
E B E K T H C A M G Q N A I N R S I F T
C H N L E R M R Y H W E H T U O T D I C
T V S G C O E G E V I A T Y I E S E C O
I G I V B U R V X A M A T I S O N R A N
O I O U Y T U D N W T S E E C U N S F F
N U N A M E K W A O L I S P R T S C G E
G X U N T V P S V Z C M O L N S W F D S
B R O T H E R H O O D T X N L F O O G S
Q U I T N E M E G D U J M L M O O A Q I
L R C Q A N W Q Z D W G C W E L C G B O
O E R A I S I N G D E A D R F X D E P N
V A P E A W D R Q J H Y H T P F X U T E
E S H N R A N O P E C N A R E V I L E D
Z K N P I H S D N E I R F Y X P F X X R
A A T I N T E R C E S S I O N X F P M O
M P S A L O S M B E A T I T U D E S K N
```

WORD LIST

CREATION	BROTHERHOOD
TRANSLATION	COMFORT
PARTING WATERS	DELIVERANCE
MANNA	DIVINITY
ASCENSION	DUTY
RESURRECTION	FAITH
BACKSLIDERS	FLOOD
BEATITUDES	FRIENDSHIP
CONFESSION	CONVERTS
PRAYER	JUDGEMENT
LOVE	INTERCESSION

Precious Metals and Stones

```
G W V N V R O A Y G E S G J A C I N T H
O C E I E D I L N T A S T E P H A K A S
L O C V U R T S A N A N Z Z A C H G X E
D M L A M G S G E R E P S A J A I Y M A
I I B E T S A O L E A N G E P L N E E E
S B E R H U E R P L A T I U M O A L I T
Z A E C E C R Y L E C O R A D X T L E I
S P A M B M I Q E J N H T R Q Y W I R L
C V N G E E D G U N A P A T C H R Y S O
A H K A R R I D N O T S S L O S I L H S
P H R E N I A S A N I N C R C U U L O Y
E V T Y O N X L E S N S R I T E P E M R
A C L T S C U T D E I T E G N S D R T H
R O Y U N O C H R I S L I N E T S O R C
L L R S A R P H S A P P H I R E U T N T
G A E E O A G R E U T I L Q U I N T E Y
O R B H U L I G A P A M E T H Y S T U Y
B N T B E X R Y L S P U W V O N V E B P
X A Y D C E D P I A E M O N E X D U Y O
Y N O X G C A R N E L I A N M U R N O N
```

WORD LIST

AGATE	JACINTH
AMETHYST	JASPER
BERYL	ONYX
CARNELIAN	PEARL
CHALCEDONY	RUBY
CHRYSOPRASE	SAPPHIRE
CHRYSOLITE	SARDONYX
CORAL	SILVER
EMERALD	TOPAZ
GOLD	TURQUOISE

About the Israelites

```
A W E S E H A D E K K A M M H E B R O N
U A G K T N T P L E D D W O O C I R S T
T M L G A P H E K S I U P R K E D E S H
A N O N F T W Z A P U L D E F B E F N O
P R N A G J E R U S A L E M G L B P L E
P A G P B C D L A N D A A O P I I C H L
U S L D A N J U P I O M F C D A R E F A
A F S I N C B A R K N M W Y H G Z O N S
H O F F B W S H R A A R A D L I T E D H
J G P L G N I H F M E F N O E A S P L A
K N E J T J A L A D U L P L H E P H E R
N O F W L G E H I P L T J O S H K I N O
L G E P L K I R N O H G H F O G F R L N
M E G I D D O B I R N E Y E P E K B R E
N D I A O M N R W C E B U H A Z O R N O
S E J P N A I P L G H T E T A E N I N G
H R N O S D K S P W R O P T E R G D L P
G I K O H O R M A H D O E N H D E D O T
P L N O F N S W O R N D F B W E N F E R
T I R Z A H P L T A A N A C H O L F A I
```

WORD LIST

JERUSALEM	GEDER	HEPHER
JARMUTH	LIBNAH	TAANACH
DEBIR	TAPPUAH	TIRZAH
ARAD	HAZOR	HEBRON
BETHEL	KEDESH	GEZER
MADON	AI	HORMAH
MEGIDDO	EGLON	MAKKEDAH
JERICHO	APHEK	LASHARON
LACHISH	ADULLAM	DOR

The Untouchables

Find the animals that were not to be eaten by the Israelites.

```
T T H P S S T L L E W T H K R O T S V
O V N C I W E S C R A E K N N P S H O
R X I D A H A O C N B E A O F E H M L
T U N S I M V N S H R E H S E B V Y C
O E H E I W E K K A A L S E A A A A
I S R A X E Z L I E T M W S L L G U R
S O R Z W R T E N E D L E Z D I T L N
E C U X W K T H K H A A W L S H A U E
S E R U T L U V L H A N S A E T S N O
S E U O L C C T H T Z R O F B O S X S
F O W Z E E O F I O E C E P Y Z N N E
L D A Y S U C N G N O H E R O N C E F
B C O U M T D H E E R P T O O O N D E
H A O C O S I L L Y T C O C A I T U R
O M U T O R L W U R C S D E W R Y F R
T T S P O I N W T C H R C S N X E S E
T A B A T S Z C O C A E L I V L I N T
M Y A N G E L L A Z M L O M O T O E L
E I K T C E V E I O V I L M S M Y F I
K I T E T I L L W E P E L I C A N E L
```

WORD LIST

TORTOISE	LIZARD	CONEY
MOLE	SWINE	CHAMELEON
HARE	HAWK	SNAILS
STORK	RAVEN	OWLS
SKINK	BATS	HERON
KITE	SWAN	WEASEL
PELICAN	CAMEL	HOOPOE
VULTURES	EAGLE	
FERRET	MOUSE	

Patriarchs, Leaders, and Sons

Unscramble the word with the given clue.

1. Had a covenant with God. AMABRAH _____

2. Rachel and Jacob's son. NINJABEM _____

3. One of twelve Israelite spies sent to Canaan and allowed to enter the promised land. CABLE _____

4. Fought the Philistine giant and won. VIADD _____

5. Through God, he challenged 45 prophets of Baal. JELAHI _____

6. Is in heaven, hallowed be his name. THERAF _____

7. Judge of Israel who needed a fleece to help confirm call from God. NEODIG _____

8. His life with prostitute wife paralleled Israel's unfaithfulness to God. ESHOA _____

9. Sarah's long-awaited son. ACSAI _____

10. Succeeded Moses. SHOJUA _____

11. Cursed by Noah to be the lowest of slaves. ANNACA _____

12. Physician author of a New Testament book. KULE _____

13. His donkey talked to him. LAMBAA _____

14. Left-handed Israelite judge. HUED _____

15. Tangled with Philistine woman with disasterous consequences. MASONS _____

Jacob's Blessings

Unscramble the word with the given clue. (Genesis 49)

1. Jacob's firstborn.   ENUBER   _____

2. Descendants should be scattered in lands given to Judah because of his violent nature.   IMOSEN   _____

3. Descendants were to be rulers and ultimately fulfilled by Christ's coming.   DUJAH   _____

4. A raw-boned donkey lying down between two saddlebags.
   CHARISSA   _____

5. Descendants were promised land by the seashore.
   ZULUNEB   _____

6. A ravenous wolf who devours prey in morning and divides plunder in evening.   JAMINBEN   _____

7. Descendant will provide justice for his people.
   AND   _____

8. His land will be bountiful and food plentiful.   SHEAR   _____

9. Will be attacked by band of raiders.   DAG   _____

10. Is a doe set free that bears beautiful fawns.
    PANTHAIL   _____

11. Descendants should be scattered among many towns of Israel because of his anger and cruelty.   VEIL   _____

12. The prince among his brothers received a great blessing.
    SHOPEJ   _____

Title Gibberish

Unscramble the word to find a book of the Bible.

1. Contains the accounts of Balaam's experiences with a donkey, Moab and prophecies.   BRUMENS   _____

2. A major prophet book.   HIAAIS   _____

3. Tells of apostles' ministry and introduces Paul.   CAST   _____

4. Book written to him by Paul because he was a strong Christian leader.   SUITT   _____

5. Old Testament book of seven chapters.   CHAMI   _____

6. Contains wise sayings mostly attributed to Solomon.   SPORBVER   _____

7. An epistle of Paul.   SLAINTAGA   _____

8. Julius Caesar was an emperor of these people.   NOMARS   _____

9. This prophet saw a wheel in a wheel.   ELIZEKE   _____

10. Tells of Babylonian captivity and the fiery furnace.   NEILAD   _____

11. Thirty-fourth book in Bible.   UNHAM   _____

12. Prayers of David.   SLAMPS   _____

13. Main character and wife of Persian king.   RESETH   _____

14. Last book of Bible.   ALEVERTION   _____

Mix 'Em Up

Unscramble the word to determine the lady.

1. Prostitute who hid two Israelite spies and saved their lives.
   HABAR _____

2. Woman judge of Israel.   HARBODE _____

3. Mother of Samuel.   NAHHAN _____

4. Israelite queen, wife of King Xerxes.   THERES _____

5. David's daughter raped by brother. (2 Samuel 13:14)
   AMART _____

6. Married husband's brother and had daughter ask for John the
   Baptist's head. (Mark 6:17)   SHIADERO _____

7. Servant and Christian sympathizer who met Peter at the door after
   his release from prison.   HADOR _____

8. Daughter of Jacob violated by Shechem. (Genesis 34:1, 2)
   NAHID _____

9. Queen of Ethiopia.   CADANCE _____

10. Mother of Gad and Asher and Leah's servant. (Genesis 35:26)
    LIPHAZ _____

11. Midian wife of Moses.   PHAROZIP _____

12. Ruth's mother-in-law.   IMOAN _____

13. Killed General Sisera. (Judges 4:21)   JELA _____

14. Got leprosy for criticizing brother Moses.   IMARIM _____

15. Husband, Nabal, died prior to marriage to David.
    GABIALI _____

16. Adam's mate.   VEE _____

Not For, But Against Them

Unscramble the word with the given clue.

1. Wanted the head of John the Baptist.   SIAHEROD   _____

2. Roman tentmaker who persecuted Christians prior to his conversion.
   LAUS   _____

3. Jewish high court where Jesus was tried.
   DRINANSHE   _____

4. Ordered execution of prophets.   BEJZELE   _____

5. Roman governor who tried Jesus.   PLATEI   _____

6. This Jewish high priest and elders plotted the arrest and death of
   Jesus.   CHAPSAIA   _____

7. Betrayed Jesus with a kiss.   SAJUD   _____

8. Paranoid king afraid of Jesus' birth.   HODER   _____

9. Ultimate evil entity.   STANA   _____

10. Egyptian king who stood against Moses.   APHORAH   _____

11. Woman who betrayed Samson.   LILEHAD   _____

12. Giant Philistine who challenged David.   OLIGHTA   _____

On the Road With Jesus

Unscramble the words to find places Jesus traveled.

1. Birthplace of Jesus.   THEBELMEH   _____

2. Mary and Joseph returned here after exodus to Egypt.
    THARAZEN   _____

3. River Jesus was baptized in.   RODJAN   _____

4. Place arrested.   THESEMANGE   _____

5. Blind Bartimaeus given sight by Jesus here.
    CHIOJER   _____

6. Home of Jesus' friends, Mary, Martha, and Lazarus.
    THANBEY   _____

7. Water changed to wine at the wedding here.
    ANAC   _____

8. Talked to woman at Jacob's well in this place.
    AMARISA   _____

9. Was crucified in this city.   SALEMJERU   _____

10. Divine home of Jesus.   VEAHEN   _____

11. Peter's mother-in-law healed by Jesus here.
     NEARMACPU   _____

12. Place of temporary refuge to escape danger while a child.
     TEPGY   _____

13. Tempted by Satan here.   TERSED   _____

14. The 5000 fed near here.   SADBATHEI   _____

Honor Thy Father and Live Long

Use the clue to find the persons who lived beyond 100 years. (Genesis 5 through 11)

1. Lived 930 years   DAMA   _____

2. Lived 962 years   EDJAR   _____

3. Lived 969 years   HALTUSEHEM   _____

4. Lived 905 years   SHEON   _____

5. Lived 950 years   AHNO   _____

6. Lived 912 years   THES   _____

7. Lived 910 years   NANEK   _____

8. Lived 777 years   CHAMLE   _____

9. Walked with God, lived 365 years   NOCHE   _____

10. Lived 895 years   MALAHALEL   _____

11. Lived 205 years   HEART   _____

12. Lived at least 500 years   HEMS   _____

Creative Jobs or Talents

Find the hidden occupation or talent.

1. Occupation of Joseph	RTEPCARNE	_____
2. Occupation of Andrew	HERMANSIF	_____
3. Talent of David	CUSIMANI	_____
4. Occupation of Demetrius	RVIHISMTSLE	_____
5. Occupation of Alexander	WORLETMAKER	_____
6. Occupation of Aquila	MKTETAERN	_____
7. Occupation of Zacchaeus (2 words)	TACLETOCLOXR	_____
8. Occupation of Elijah	THOPPER	_____
9. Gideon's claim to fame	DUJEG	_____
10. Occupation of Nicodemus	ISEEPHAR	_____
11. Joseph was this to dreams	PRETRENEIRT	_____
12. Joshua was this to the Israelites	DEALER	_____

Abraham's Relatives

Unscramble the word to find the hidden relative.

1. Also known as Israel. JOBAC _____

2. Promised son of covenant. CASIA _____

3. Child born before the promised son. SHEMAIL _____

4. Abraham's second wife. KATHURE _____

5. Son of Esau and Adah. PHAZELI _____

6. Abraham's wife. HARAS _____

7. Abraham's wife's maid. GRAHA _____

8. Favorite wife of Israel. LREACH _____

9. Firstborn of Leah. UNBERE _____

10. Sold birthright to brother. SEAU _____

11. Son of Israel and Pharaoh confidant. SHOJEP _____

12. Daughter of Leah. HANID _____

13. Abraham's birth name. BRAMA _____

14. Mother named him Ben-Oni. INJAMBEN _____

A Numbers Thing

Unscramble the word to find the correct number.

1. Number of apostles.   WETLEV   ~~twelve~~ 12 ~~twelve~~ *twelve*

2. Esau and Jacob as twins equaled this.   WOT   *Two*

3. Number of commandments given to Moses.   NET   *Ten*

4. Number of years Satan to be bound in bottomless pit. (Revelation 20:2)   SOUTHDAN   *thousand*

5. Number of times Peter denied Christ.   THERE   *three*

6. Number of loaves of bread used to feed the 5000.   VIFE   *Five*

7. Number of churches mentioned in Revelation.   EVENS   _____

8. Number of thieves crucified with Christ.   TOW   *Two*

9. Number of days of the great flood.   TROFY   *Forty*

10. Number of books in the Bible.   XISYT-XIS   *Sixty-six*

11. Number of angels that will stand on corners of the earth holding winds. (Revelation 7:1)   FURO   *Your*

12. Number of pieces of silver paid for betraying Christ.   TRITHY   *thirty*

13. Number of years added to Hezekiah's life after he prayed. (2 Kings 20:6)   TEENFIF   *Fifteen*

14. Number of fruits of the spirit. (Galatians 5:16-26)   NENI   *nine*

15. Number of God's begotten sons.   EON   *One*

A Ram in the Bulrushes

God had a ram hidden in the bushes for Abraham when he was going to sacrifice Isaac. The word "RAM" is hidden in the following missing words. There may be spaces between the letters. Use the descriptor to guess the word. The location of the letters "RAM" are indicated.

1. Father of Hebrews   __ __ RAM

2. Father of Moses and Aaron (Numbers 26:59)   __ __ RAM

3. Son of Shem (Genesis10:22)   __ RAM

4. Joseph's second son (Genesis 41:52; 46:20)   __ __ __ RA __ M

5. King of Tyre, friend of David (2 Samuel 5:11)   __ __ RAM

6. A king of Judah, Jehoshaphat's son
   (2 Kings 1:17)   __ __ __ __ RAM

7. Sister of Moses   __ __ R __ AM

8. Clothing   RA __ M __ __ __ __

9. King of Gezer (Joshua 10:33)   __ __ RAM

10. One of the seven churches in Asia
   (Revelation 1:11)   __ __ R __ AM __ __

11. Visions during sleep   __ R __ AM

12. Hebrew-built treasure city (Exodus 1:11)   RAM __ __ __ __

13. Son of Benjamin (Numbers 26:38)   __ __ __ RAM

14. To enclose or skeleton   __ RAM __

Eli, Eli

Each of the following words contain the word ELI in its spelling. Don't be confused by any spaces between the letters. Use the descriptor and decipher the word. The location of the letters "ELI" are indicated.

1. Challenged the prophets of Baal on
   Mt. Carmel and had a death
   sentence placed on him by Jezebel.
   (1 Kings 17—19)   ELI __ __ __

2. Witnessed the translation of his friend
   and fellow prophet. (2 Kings 2:11, 12)   ELI __ __ __

3. Twenty-first book of the Bible.   E __ __ L __ __ I __ __ __ __ __

4. One who has received Christ.   __ ELI __ __ __ __

5. Descendants of Jacob   __ __ __ __ ELI __ __ __

6. "I sought the Lord, and he answered
   me, and _____ me from all my
   fears." (Psalm 34:4)   __ ELI __ __ __ __ __

7. Woman betrayer of Samson   __ ELI __ __ __

8. Descendants of Ishmael   __ __ __ __ __ ELI __ __ __

9. Top part of a room   __ E __ LI __ __

10. Moses' son (Exodus 18:2-4)   ELI __ __ __ __

11. Father of Bathsheba (2 Samuel 11:3)   ELI __ __

12. Wife of Zechariah, Mary's cousin   ELI __ __ __ __ __ __

13. Father of Joseph, Christ's ancestor
    (Luke 3:23)   __ ELI

14. An accused Paul was taken to this
    Roman governor.   __ ELI __

Give Ear to This Word

The ear is instrumental for listening and communication. Find the word containing the word EAR in its spelling. Use the descriptor and listen for a clue. The location of the letters "EAR" are indicated.

1. The pure in _____ shall be blessed.   __ EAR __

2. God created the heaven and the _____.   EAR __ __

3. Offered to Christ on the cross   __ __ __ E __ AR

4. Jesus went to Heaven to _____ a place for us.   __ __ E __ AR __

5. A son of Ishmael (Genesis 25:13)   __ E __ AR

6. To be afraid is to _____.   __ EAR __ __ __

7. David killed a lion and this animal for harming a lamb.   __ EAR

8. To leave   __ E __ AR __

9. A Roman ruler   __ __ E __ AR

10. Hair on a man's face   __ EAR __

11. To materialize or become visible   __ __ __ EAR

12. This was used to pierce Jesus' side.   __ __ EAR

13. To take an oath   __ __ EAR

14. Close   __ EAR

Then There Was Man

Man was made to have dominion over the inhabitants of the sea, air, and land. Use the following descriptors and find the word containing the word MAN in the missing words below. The location of the letters "MAN" are indicated.

1. Helpmate for man
      __ __ MAN

2. Oldest son of Joseph; grandson of Jacob (Genesis 41:51)
      MAN __ __ __ __ __

3. Bread of Heaven
      MAN __ __

4. Garden of Jesus' betrayal
      __ __ __ __ __ __ __ MAN __

5. First bed of Jesus; cattle feeding place
      MAN __ __ __

6. Paul was born this type of citizen.
      __ __ MAN

7. One who fishes
      __ __ __ __ __ __ MAN

8. Moses was given ten of these.
      __ __ __ MAN __ __ __ __ __ __

9. This name means God with us.
      __ __ MAN __ __ __

10. A member of the upper class
      __ __ __ __ __ MAN

11. Grandson of Benjamin; great-grandson of Jacob (1 Chronicles 8:4)
      __ __ __ MAN

12. Plotted to destroy Jews because Mordecai did not bow to him.
      __ __ MAN

13. Clothing, coat, robe
      MAN __ __ __

Female of the Species

The opposite of he is she. The female of the human species is a help-mate but also stands alone in many words. Use the following descriptors and find the word containing the word "SHE" in the missing words below. The location of the letters "SHE" are indicated.

1. Feed my _____.   SHE __ __

2. The queen of this country came
   to test Solomon.   SHE __ __

3. Covering for a knife or sword   SHE __ __ __

4. We shall come rejoicing bringing
   in the _____.   SHE __ __ __ __

5. An ancient measure of money   SHE __ __ __

6. Guardian or keeper of the flock   SHE __ __ __ __

7. Wife of David; mother of
   Solomon   __ __ __ __ SHE __ __

8. Residue from burning   __ SHE __

9. Noah's oldest son   SHE __

10. Jacob's second son by Leah's
    maid, Zilpah   __ SHE __

11. A measure of dry items, grains   __ __ SHE __

12. Aaron's wife   __ __ __ SHE __ __

It's in the Old

Across
1. Major division of the Bible.
2. God's book.
5. Son of Lot.
7. Priest and scribe and author of book with historical theme.
8. Speech; tongue.
10. A ruler and one of two Old Testament books.
12. Abbreviation of Genesis.
14. Purpose of manna.
15. Abbreviation of Micah.
16. Instructed to build an ark before the onset of the great flood.
17. Abbreviation of Habakkuk.
21. Philistine city of Delilah.
22. Book containing wise sayings of Solomon.
23. Tenth king of Israel.
24. Minor prophet preached of locust plague and of the Day of the Lord.
26. Brother of Moses.
27. Third book of the Bible attributed to Moses.

Down
1. Solomon built this great building for God.
3. Bible book named after a woman.
4. Major prophet of the Old Testament.
6. Old Testament minor prophet and author.
9. Opposite of evil.
11. Abbreviation of Jonah.
13. Book about suffering.
15. Book predicts a forerunner to prepare the way for the Messiah, Christ.
16. This identifier was changed for several people in the Bible, one was Abraham.
18. Book contains stories of the conquest of Caanan after Moses' death.
19. Abbreviation of Song of Solomon.
20. Songs are the theme of this book.
25. Abbreviation of Old Testament.

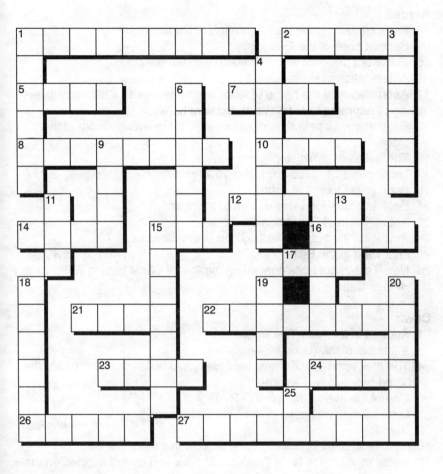

It's in the New

Across

1. Book containing the transfiguration of Christ.
2. Second book of the Gospels.
5. Followers of Christ who helped spread the gospel.
9. Abbreviation of Philippians.
11. Abbreviation of the name of letter written to Jewish Christians thinking of returning to old ways of Judaism.
13. Baby Jesus slept in a manger because there was no room at this place.
15. The duties of a minister.
17. Labor pains of childbirth. (John 16:21, KJV)
19. Book after Gospel of John.
21. Book of Third John was written to this man.
22. Abbreviation of Thessalonians.
24. Physician attributed to writing one of the Gospels.
25. Last word in the Bible.
26. New Testament book containing miracle of Christ turning water to wine at Cana.

Down

1. Authors of the New Testament.
3. A tithable plant. (Luke 11:42)
4. The rock upon which Christ said He would build His church, also the name of two New Testament books.
6. One of the twelve disciples or Paul.
7. Letters taken as books of the New Testament.
8. Non-Jews.
10. New Testament books centered around this man.
12. Wrote many of the New Testament books and was converted on the road to Damascus.
14. New Testament epistle written to Paul's friend left on the island of Crete to strengthen the Cretean church.
16. Abbreviation of last book of the Bible; it has a prophecy theme.
18. New Testament book written by brother of Jesus.
20. Abbreviation of Corinthians.
21. Abbreviation of Galatians.
22. Abbreviation of book written by Paul to Lois' grandson.
23. Abbreviation of a New Testament book that uses the church as the body of Christ as one of the themes.

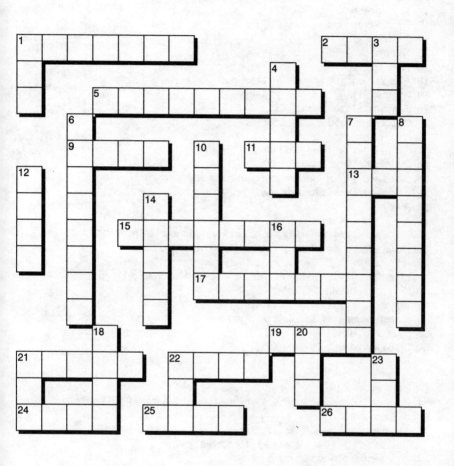

David and Solomon

Across
1. Mother of King Solomon.
5. Nephew of David who convinced Amnon to seduce his half-sister. (2 Samuel 13)
9. David wanted Uriah to do this at the forefront of battle. (2 Samuel 11)
10. David not allowed to build this but Solomon did. (1 Chronicles 22)
11. To compete.
13. To consume food.
14. Promises.
15. To help.
16. Pain.
18. A large modern-day measure of weight.
19. A regulation.
20. Something to sleep on.
21. Opposite of good.
23. Used in anointing.
27. Saul's oldest son and good friend of David.
28. Daughter of Saul and wife of David. (1 Samuel 18:20-27)
30. David was a direct descendant of this son of Adam.
31. Number of David's father's sons.
34. A being.
35. A part of the trinity.
36. David's daughter raped by her half-brother, Amnon. (2 Samuel 13)
39. David wrote many of the chapters in this book of the Bible.
41. A friend.
45. Beautiful and wise widow of Nabal and subsequent wife of David. (1 Samuel 25:3)
46. Kingdom, domain.
47. Water on the ground in early morning.
49. Eldest daughter of Saul supposed to marry David but married Adriel instead. (1 Samuel 18:17-19)
50. David's predecessor who ruled Israel.
51. An ancient coin.

Down
1. Process to cleanse the body. Bathsheba was doing this when David noticed her. (2 Samuel 11)
2. An enticement, lure.
3. David's son and the wisest king of the Israelites.
4. David and Bathsheba committed this.
5. The City of David.
6. Prophet sent to rebuke David for his actions concerning Bathsheba.
7. Second king of Israel.
8. Favored by God.
12. A young man.
17. Philistine giant defeated by David.
20. A shrub or hedge.
22. First husband of Bathsheba; warrior of David. (1 Samuel 11:3 and 2 Samuel 23:39)

24. First occupation of David.
25. This was done to a person to signify his being chosen by God.
26. Eldest brother of David.
27. Father of David.
29. A large town.
32. David left Gath to escape to this cave. (1 Samuel 22:1)
33. Instrument played by David.
37. Solomon asked for this instead of riches and honor.
38. Rahab's son. (Matthew 1:5)
40. Prophet and Hannah's son who anointed Saul as king.
42. A regulation.
43. Solomon had many of these.
44. To run.
46. Naomi's daughter-in-law and grandmother of David's father.
48. A battle of nations.

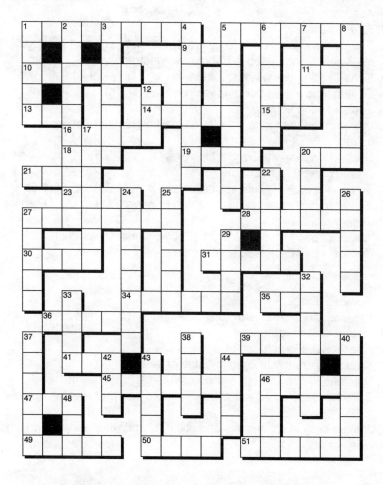

Battles

Across

1. Used by David to fight Goliath.
3. Armageddon, the final _____; a fight.
6. Jael killed Sisera in this structure. (Judges 5:20-30)
8. He brought 400 men to meet his brother, Jacob. (Genesis 32, 33)
10. To help.
13. Helped deliver Israel from Moab during the time of the judges. (Judges 3:15-30)
14. Surprise attack; Joshua's battle plan for capture and destruction of Ai. (Joshua 8:4)
15. Assembly of soldiers.
17. Parts of a navy.
18. Fire from the Lord used to destroy Sodom. (Genesis 19:24, KJV)
20. Heavenly beings used to bring mass destruction.
22. Used to bring down walls; battering ____. (Ezekiel 26:9)
24. Goliath was a member of these people.
28. Tools used in fighting.
29. Weapon made of long wooden staff with pointed or sharp metal head on top.
30. Second king of Israel and a king of war.
31. A requirement or necessity.
32. To cry. A result of great sorrow or anguish. (1 Samuel 30:1-6)
33. A treacherous being used by Isaiah to denote enemies of Palestine. (Isaiah 14:29)
34. Weapon made of long straight or curved blade with a hilt.
35. Representatives of God sometimes consulted in war.

Down

1. Surprise attack.
2. Promised to protect Israelites if obeyed and worshiped.
4. Instrument of war; battle ___.
5. Insects used in plagues of Egypt.
7. Musical instruments used in battle of Jericho.
9. David used five smooth items like these against Goliath.
11. Exiled to Babylon as war casualty; could interpret dreams. (Daniel 1:17)
12. Joshua prayed for this to stand still until the Amorites were defeated. (Joshua 10:12, 13)
16. Defeated Midianites. (Judges 7)

17. To rest at night.
19. Single-handedly destroyed thousands of Philistines.
21. These fell in Jericho battle.
23. Used for transportation by armies.
25. Men that drank water this way were used by Gideon to select an army. (Judges 7:5-7)
26. Plunder or loot from a battle.
27. To withdraw from battle or to fall back.
28. Injuries.
30. To pass away.
32. An armed conflict between nations.

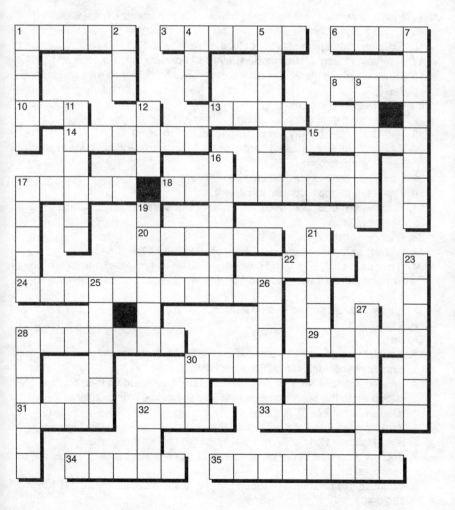

Mountain of Clues

Across
1. Place where the Ten Commandments were given.
3. "I will lift up mine eyes unto the hills, from whence cometh my ___." (Psalm 121:1, KJV)
6. These parts of mountains were seen first when the great flood waters subsided. (Genesis 8:5)
8. Way to go up a hill.
10. Jesus went up into a mountain to do this before His walk on the water. (Mark 6:38)
11. Built a boat that eventually rested on a mountain after the great flood.
15. These formed Christ's Sermon on the Mount. (Matthew 5)
16. Extreme shortage or scarcity of food.
17. Mountain of God, Moses tended Jethro's flock near this. (Exodus 3:1)
19. Mountain where the 2200 men were removed from Gideon's army. (Judges 7:3)
20. Abbreviation of elevation.
22. Shelter from danger, or sanctuary.
23. And God called the dry land ___. (Genesis 1:10, KJV)
26. Fate of those who touched border of Mt. Sinai when God gave Moses the Ten Commandments.
29. Low place between two mountains.
30. Type of deer and mountain inhabitant.
31. Place where disciples were told of end of world and coming of Christ. (Matthew 24:3)
32. A range of hills or mountains.
33. Witnessed the transfiguration of Jesus. (Matthew 17:1)
34. "They called to the ___ and the rocks, 'Fall on us and hide us from the face of him who sits on the throne and from the wrath of the Lamb!'" (Revelation 6:16)
35. Abraham's faith tested here. (Genesis 22:1-19)

Down
1. Mountain range home of Esau. (Genesis 32:3)
2. Final home of Noah's ark. (Genesis 8:4)
4. Reuben, Gad, Asher, Zebulun, Dan, and Naphtali stood on this mount to give curses when the people crossed the Jordan into the promised land. (Deuteronomy 27:13)
5. Peter, James, and John witnessed this change in Jesus on this high mountain. (Matthew 17:1)
7. God put a rainbow in the sky as this as a promise that the earth would not be destroyed by a flood.
9. Mountain site of contest between Elijah and 450 prophets of Baal. (1 Kings 18:20-40)

12. Mountain near Jericho where Moses viewed land of Canaan. (Deuteronomy 32:49)
13. The mountain did this when the Lord descended upon it before giving Moses the Commandments. (Exodus 19:18, KJV)
14. Abbreviation of Genesis.
18. Site of Abraham's altar in Canaan. (Genesis 13:3, 4)
21. Covered everything during great flood.
23. Joseph's second son.
24. "Confessing their sins, they were baptized by him in the Jordan _____." (Mark 1:5)
25. Peter said this to Jesus on the mountain during the transfiguration: "It is good for us to be ___." (Matthew 17:4)
27. An opening in a side of a mountain. Lot and his daughters stayed in one after destruction of Sodom and Gomorrah. (Genesis 19:30)
28. Moses viewed promised land from top of this. (Deuteronomy 3:27)

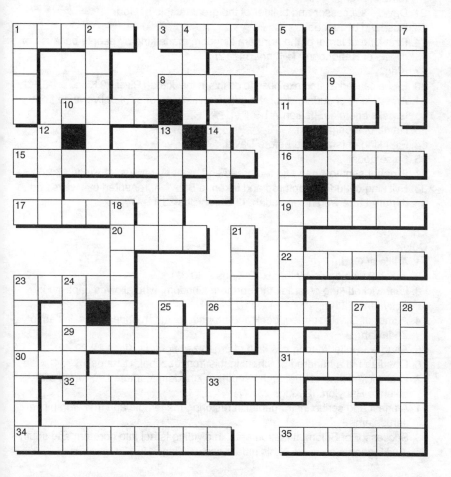

Kings and Kings

Across

1. The southern kingdom of ancient Israel.
4. Ahab's evil wife. (1 Kings 16:31)
8. One who serves others.
9. Second king of united Israel.
10. Kings were usually this.
12. King Josiah had this holy item, which supposedly contained Ten Commandments, put back into Solomon's temple. (2 Chronicles 35:3)
14. Name belonging to both a king of Israel and a prophet to a king of Judah.
16. Foreign queen who came to test and question Solomon. (1 Kings 10:1-13)
17. Elijah prayed for this water to fall from clouds.
20. His seven days was the shortest period of a ruler in the northern kingdom of Israel. (1 Kings 16:9-20)
21. David's successor and builder of the great temple of God.
23. Husband of Jezebel.
24. First king of Israel of the northern kingdom made king by people because of dislike of Rehoboam. (1 Kings 11, 12)
27. King.
30. Elisha caused an iron axe head to do this in the Jordan River. (2 Kings 6:1-6, KJV)
31. An evil king of Judah who refused Isaiah's divine offer of deliverance from Israel's enemies. (Isaiah 7:1-9)
33. Name of a pagan god.
34. First king of Israel and before David.
35. False gods.
37. Prophet sent to Ahab and fed bread and meat by ravens. (1 Kings 17:2-7)
38. Evil king of Judah, captured and taken to Babylon, repented evil ways and restored true worship in Judah. (2 Chronicles 33:11-17)

Down

1. A title of God.
2. Jezebel was eaten by these. (2 Kings 9:30-37)
3. Last wicked king of Israel, the northern kingdom, who allowed captivity by Assyrians. (2 Kings 17:1-6)
4. Author of Old Testament book and prophet to Judah under kings Josiah to Zedekiah.
5. Ahab was killed during this kind of organized fight. (1 Kings 22:29-40)
6. Obadiah hid a hundred prophets in this from Jezebel. (1 Kings 18:3, 4)
7. Last wicked king of Judah, the southern kingdom; captured, tortured, and taken to Babylon. (2 Kings 25:1-7)
11. A priest and scribe instrumental in restoring the temple and true worship in Jerusalem.
13. Successor of Solomon instrumental in dividing Israel into northern and southern kingdoms because of his unfairness. (1 Kings 12)

15. Prophet and successor to Elijah who performed miracles.
18. Name of the northern kingdom.
19. Abbreviation of kings.
22. Ritual involving a burnt offering to atone for a sin.
24. Righteous and last good king of Judah, crowned when 8 years old, reigning 31 years, prepared temple and restored true worship. (2 Kings 22:1, 2)
25. Daughter of Jezebel who usurped the throne of Judah to become queen for 6 years. (2 Kings 8, 11)
26. Righteous king of Judah who reigned 52 years but was punished with leprosy for trying to assume a priestly function in the temple of the Lord. (2 Chronicles 26)
28. Opposite of good.
29. Main reference book on God's word, ancient kings of Israel, and prophets.
32. Esther's husband's kingdom included people from many of these.
36. Third and generally good king of Judah, overthrew idolatry and defeated the Ethiopians. (2 Chronicles 14)

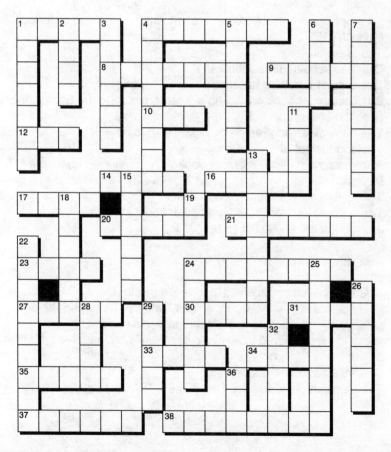

The Messiah

Across

1. Birthplace of Jesus Christ.
3. Jesus was prophecied to be born of this.
5. Man should do this continuously.
6. Peter did this three times before the rooster crowed when asked about knowing Jesus.
8. Wise men followed this in the sky in search of Jesus.
9. ___a, the son of Menna and ancestor of Jesus. (Luke 3:31)
10. Opposite of life.
12. John described Jesus as the ___ of the world. (John 8:12)
13. "Repent ___: for the kingdom of heaven is at hand." (Matthew 3:2, KJV)
14. Soldiers at the cross gambled for Jesus' garments by casting these. (Luke 23:34)
16. An act.
17. As prophecied these were not broken when Jesus was crucified. (John 19:36)
18. The Messiah.
21. Crushed in spirit or heartbroken.
24. Opposite of a truth, a falsehood.
25. Old Testament book predicting a forerunner, John the Baptist, to pre-ceed the Messiah.
27. The book of Isaiah predicted the Messiah to be heir to the throne of this king. (Isaiah 9:7)
28. Abbreviation of Old Testament book with prophecies about the Messiah.
30. Two of these were crucified with Jesus.
31. The book of Zechariah had prediction about the _____ body of Jesus. (Zechariah 12:10; 13:6)

Down

1. Double-crossed or deceived, Judas did this to Jesus.
2. When Jesus was very young, Joseph was told through a dream to take Mary and Jesus to this country to avoid danger.
3. Wine ___ was offered to Jesus to drink while on the cross. (Matthew 27:48)
4. Jesus sentenced to die on this.
6. The Messiah came to offer this. (Luke 4:18, KJV)

7. The prophet ___jah was seen with Jesus during the transfiguration. (Matthew 17:3)
11. Jesus said, "___ and you will receive." (John 16:24)
15. He killed many innocent children to find the Messiah. (Matthew 2:16)
18. Led the soldiers to capture Jesus.
19. Thirty pieces of this were paid for the selling of the Messiah.
20. Appeared.
21. This liquid was shed by Jesus for our sins.
22. He will baptize you with the ___ Spirit and with fire. (Matthew 3:11)
23. The descendants of Judah formed one of these.
26. Without sight.
29. Abbreviation of Isaiah.

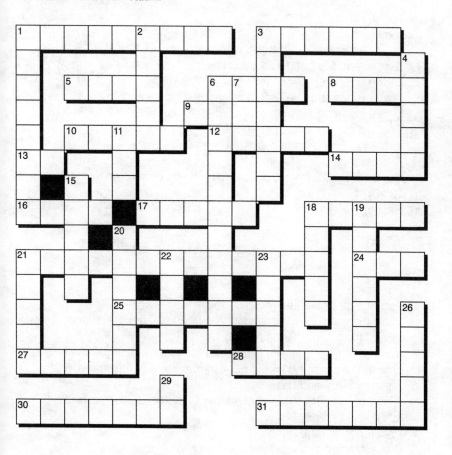

Hodgepodge

Across

1. "The ____r shall serve the younger." (Romans 9:12, KJV)
5. Name Naomi gave herself. Ruth 1:20.
9. Sent by Ezra with others to Iddo with a message. (Ezra 8:16, 17)
10. First man on earth.
11. A heavy weight.
12. Intense anger.
13. Town of Benjamin which was rebuilt by Shemed. (1 Chronicles 8:12)
14. Opposite of women.
15. "Thou hast delivered me from the ___ngs of the people." (Psalm 18:43, KJV)
19. Past tense of hide.
20. ___o, An Egyptian Pharaoh who killed Josiah. (2 Kings 23:29, 30)
21. Evening or day before a special event, day, or holiday.
23. Of the earth.
27. "You prepare a table before me in the presence of my enemies. You ___int my head with oil; my cup overflows." (Psalm 23:5)
28. The last supper was in the upper ____m.
29. Timothy's grandmother. (2 Timothy 1:5)
31. A messenger.
34. "No one takes it from me, but I lay it down of my own ____rd." (John 10:18)
35. Past tense of arise.
36. To scatter or spill.
37. To crush.

Down

1. A mistake.
2. Top of a jar or basket.
3. "Now the earth was formless and empty, darkness was over the surface of the ___p." (Genesis 1:2)
4. "Even though ___athan, Delaiah, and Gemariah, urged the king not to burn the scroll, he would not listen to them." (Jeremiah 36:25)
5. Sister of Mary and Lazarus, _____tha.
6. A part of the border of the children of Naphtali. (Joshua 19:32, 33, KJV)
7. Past tense of rage.
8. So be it; ending of a prayer.
9. Your mother's sister.
11. Supervisor.

16. W___, made from grapes.
17. Moses put a __il over his face after talking with God on Mt. Sinai.
18. Frozen water.
19. Mountain site of Aaron's death. (Numbers 20:25-28)
21. Son of Cain.
22. Used in speaking or singing.
24. Refuse, garbage.
25. "Foxes have _____s and birds of the air have nests." (Matthew 8:20)
26. Tenth letter of Hebrew alphabet.
27. Exclamation of unhappiness or intense sorrow.
30. Dirt.
31. Son of Noah.
32. A period of time.
33. "I am a ___e of Sharon, a lily of the valleys." (Song of Solomon 2:1)

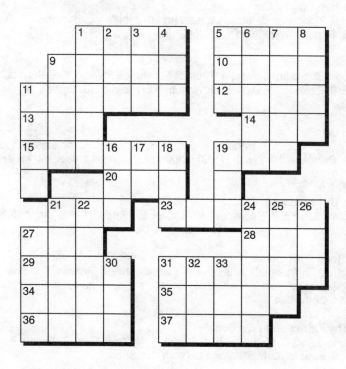

Answers

Generations
1. D, 2. H, 3. I, 4. A, 5. J, 6. B, 7. C, 8. F, 9. G, 10. E.

Siblings (Half or Otherwise)
1. B, 2. G, 3. J, 4. P, 5. H, 6. N, 7. A, 8. Q, 9. D, 10. I, 11. C, 12. O, 13. M, 14. L, 15. E, 16. F, 17. K.

It's About Africa
1. C, 2. E, 3. G, 4. A, 5. B, 6. H, 7. I, 8. J, 9. D, 10. F.

Patriarchs, Leaders, and Sons
1. Abraham, 2. Benjamin, 3. Caleb, 4. David, 5. Elijah, 6. Father, 7. Gideon, 8. Hosea, 9. Isaac, 10. Joshua, 11. Canaan, 12. Luke, 13. Balaam, 14. Ehud, 15. Samson.

Jacob's Blessings
1. Reuben, 2. Simeon, 3. Judah, 4. Issachar, 5. Zebulun, 6. Benjamin, 7. Dan, 8. Asher, 9. Gad, 10. Naphtali, 11. Levi, 12. Joseph.

Title Gibberish
1. Numbers, 2. Isaiah, 3. Acts, 4. Titus, 5. Micah, 6. Proverbs, 7. Galatians, 8. Romans, 9. Ezekiel, 10. Daniel, 11. Nahum, 12. Psalms, 13. Esther, 14. Revelation.

Mix 'Em Up
1. Rahab, 2. Deborah, 3. Hannah, 4. Esther, 5. Tamar, 6. Herodias, 7. Rhoda, 8. Dinah, 9. Candace, 10. Zilpah, 11. Zipporah, 12. Naomi, 13. Jael, 14. Miriam, 15. Abigail, 16. Eve.

Not For, But Against Them
1. Herodias, 2. Saul, 3. Sanhedrin, 4. Jezebel, 5. Pilate, 6. Caiaphas, 7. Judas, 8. Herod, 9. Satan, 10. Pharaoh, 11. Delilah, 12. Goliath.

On the Road With Jesus
1. Bethlehem, 2. Nazareth, 3. Jordan, 4. Gethsemane, 5. Jericho, 6. Bethany, 7. Cana, 8. Samaria, 9. Jerusalem, 10. Heaven, 11. Capernaum, 12. Egypt, 13. Desert, 14. Bethsaida.

Honor Thy Father and Live Long
1. Adam, 2. Jared, 3. Methuselah, 4. Enosh, 5. Noah, 6. Seth, 7. Kenan, 8. Lamech, 9. Enoch, 10. Mahalalel, 11. Terah, 12. Shem.

Creative Jobs or Talents
1. Carpenter, 2. Fisherman, 3. Musician, 4. Silversmith, 5. Metalworker, 6. Tentmaker, 7. Tax Collector, 8. Prophet, 9. Judge, 10. Pharisee, 11. Interpreter, 12. Leader.

Abraham's Relatives

1. Jacob, 2. Isaac, 3. Ishmael, 4. Keturah, 5. Eliphaz, 6. Sarah, 7. Hagar, 8. Rachel, 9. Reuben, 10. Esau, 11. Joseph, 12. Dinah, 13. Abram, 14. Benjamin.

A Numbers Thing

1. Twelve, 2. Two, 3. Ten, 4. Thousand, 5. Three, 6. Five, 7. Seven, 8. Two, 9. Forty, 10. Sixty-six, 11. Four, 12. Thirty, 13. Fifteen, 14. Nine, 15. One.

A Ram in the Bulrushes

1. Abram, 2. Amram, 3. Aram, 4. Ephraim, 5. Hiram, 6. Jehoram, 7. Miriam, 8. Raiments, 9. Horam, 10. Pergamum, 11. Dream, 12. Rameses, 13. Ahiram, 14. Frame.

Eli, Eli

1. Elijah, 2. Elisha, 3. Ecclesiastes, 4. Believer, 5. Israelites, 6. Delivered, 7. Delilah, 8. Ishmaelites, 9. Ceiling, 10. Eliezer, 11. Eliam, 12, Elizabeth, 13. Heli, 14. Felix.

Give Ear to This Word

1. Heart, 2. Earth, 3. Vinegar, 4. Prepare, 5. Kedar, 6. Feareth, 7. Bear, 8. Depart, 9. Caesar, 10. Beard, 11. Appear, 12. Spear, 13. Swear, 14. Near.

Then There Was Man

1. Woman, 2. Manasseh, 3. Manna, 4. Gethsemane, 5. Manger, 6. Roman, 7. Fisherman, 8. Commandments, 9. Immanuel, 10. Nobleman, 11. Naaman, 12. Haman, 13. Mantle.

Female of the Species

1. Sheep, 2. Sheba, 3. Sheath, 4. Sheaves, 5. Shekel, 6. Shepherd, 7. Bathsheba, 8. Ashes, 9. Shem, 10. Asher, 11. Bushel, 12. Elisheba.

It's in the Old

Across: 1. Testament, 2. Bible, 5. Moab, 7. Ezra, 8. Language, 10. King, 12. Gen, 14. Food, 15. Mic, 16. Noah, 17. Hab, 21. Gaza, 22. Proverbs, 23. Jehu, 24. Joel, 26. Aaron, 27. Leviticus. **Down:** 1. Temple, 3. Esther, 4. Ezekiel, 6. Haggai, 9. Good, 11. Jon, 13. Job, 15. Malachi, 16. Name, 18. Joshua, 19. Song, 20. Psalms, 25. OT.

It's in the New

Across: 1. Matthew, 2. Mark, 5. Disciples, 9. Phil, 11. Heb, 13. Inn, 15. Ministry, 17. Travail, 19. Acts, 21. Gaius, 22. Thes, 24. Luke, 25. Amen, 26. John, **Down:** 1. Men, 3. Rue, 4. Peter, 6. Apostles, 7. Epistles, 8. Gentiles, 10. Christ, 12. Paul, 14. Titus, 16. Rev, 18. Jude, 20. Cor, 21. Gal, 22. Tim, 23. Eph.

David and Solomon

Across: 1. Bathsheba, 5. Jonadab, 9. Die, 10. Temple, 11. Vie, 13. Eat, 14. Oaths, 15. Aid, 16. Agony, 18. Ton, 19. Rule, 20. Bed, 21. Evil, 23. Oils, 27. Jonathan, 28. Michal, 30. Seth, 31. Eight, 34. Entity, 35. God, 36. Tamar, 39. Psalms, 41. Pal, 45. Abigail, 46. Realm, 47. Dew, 49. Merab, 50. Saul, 51.

Shekel. **Down:** 1. Bathe, 2. Temptation, 3. Solomon, 4. Adultery, 5. Jerusalem, 6. Nathan, 7. David, 8. Blessed, 12. Boy, 17. Goliath, 20. Bush, 22. Uriah, 24. Shepherd, 25. Anoint, 26. Eliab, 27. Jesse, 29. City, 32. Adullam, 33. Harp, 37. Wisdom, 38. Boaz, 40. Samuel, 42. Law, 43. Wives, 44. Flee, 46. Ruth, 48. War.

Battles
Across: 1. Sling, 3. Battle, 6. Tent, 8. Esau, 10. Aid, 13. Ehud, 14. Ambush, 15. Troop, 17. Ships, 18. Brimstone, 20. Angels, 22. Ram, 24. Philistines, 28. Weapons, 29. Spear, 30. David, 31. Need, 32. Weep, 33. Serpent, 34. Sword, 35. Prophets. **Down:** 1. Sneak, 2. God, 4. Axe, 5. Locusts, 7. Trumpets, 9. Stones, 11. Daniel, 12. Sun, 16. Gideon, 17. Sleep, 19. Samson, 21. Walls, 23. Chariot, 25. Lapped, 26. Spoils, 27. Retreat, 28. Wounds, 30. Die, 32. War.

Mountain of Clues
Across: 1. Sinai, 3. Help, 6. Tops, 8. Walk. 10. Pray, 11. Noah, 15. Beatitudes, 16. Famine, 17. Horeb, 19. Gilead, 20. Elev, 22. Refuge, 23. Earth, 26. Death, 29. Valley, 30. Roe, 31. Olives, 32. Ridge, 33. John, 34. Mountains, 35. Moriah. **Down:** 1. Seir, 2. Ararat, 4. Ebal, 5. Transfiguration, 7. Sign, 9. Carmel, 12. Nebo, 13. Quake, 14. Gen, 18. Bethel, 21. Water, 23. Ephraim, 24. River, 25. Here, 27. Cave, 28. Pisgah.

Kings and Kings
Across: 1. Judah, 4. Jezebel, 8. Servant, 9. David, 10. Men, 12. Ark, 14. Jehu, 16. Sheba, 17. Rain, 20. Zimri, 21. Solomon, 23. Ahab, 24. Jeroboam, 27. Ruler, 30. Swim, 31. Ahaz, 33. Baal, 34. Saul, 35. Idols, 37. Elijah, 38. Manasseh. **Down:** 1. Jehovah, 2. Dogs, 3. Hoshea, 4. Jeremiah, 5. Battle, 6. Cave, 7. Zedekiah, 11. Ezra, 13. Rehoboam, 15. Elisha, 18. Israel, 19. Ki, 22. Sacrifice, 24. Josiah, 25. Athaliah, 26. Uzziah, 28. Evil, 29. Bible, 32. Lands, 36. Asa.

The Messiah
Across: 1. Bethlehem, 3. Virgin, 5. Pray, 6. Deny, 8. Star, 9. Mele, 10. Death, 12. Light, 13. Ye, 14. Lots, 16. Deed, 17. Bones, 18. Jesus, 21. Brokenhearted, 24. Lie, 25. Malachi, 27. David, 28. Zech, 30. Thieves, 31. Pierced. **Down:** 1. Betrayed, 2. Egypt, 3. Vinegar, 4. Cross, 6. Deliverance, 7. Eli, 11. Ask, 15. Herod, 18. Judas, 19. Silver, 20. Seemed, 21. Blood, 22. Holy, 23. Tribe, 26. Blind, 29. Is.

Hodgepodge
Across: 1. Elde, 5. Mara, 9. Ariel, 10. Adam, 11. Burden, 12. Rage, 13. Ono, 14. Men, 15. Strivi, 19. Hid, 20. Nec, 21. Eve, 23. Earthy, 27. Ano, 28. Roo, 29. Lois, 31. Herald, 34. Acco, 35. Arose, 36. Shed, 37. Mash. **Down:** 1. Error, 2. Lid, 3. Dee, 4. Eln, 5. Mar, 6. Adami, 7. Raged, 8. Amen, 9. Aunt, 11. Boss, 16. Ine, 17. Ve, 19. Hor, 21. Enoch, 22. Voice, 24. Trash, 25. Hole, 26. Yod, 27. Alas, 30. Sod, 31. Ham, 32. Era, 33. Ros.